Desert Graces

Meditations Inspired by the Sonoran Desert

Rev. Thomas M. Santa, C.Ss.R.

E.T. NEDDER PUBLISHING

Cover and book design by Sharon Nicki and by Lynn Else, Paulist Press

Library of Congress Cataloging-in-Publication Data

Santa, Thomas M., 1952–
    Desert graces : meditations inspired by the Sonoran Desert / Thomas M. Santa.
        p. cm.
    ISBN 978-1-893757-63-9 (alk. paper)
    1. Spirituality—Catholic Church. 2. Spirituality—United States. 3. Catholic Church—Prayers and devotions. 4. Deserts—Religious aspects—Christianity. 5. Nature—Religious aspects—Christianity. 6. Sonoran Desert—Miscellanea. I. Title.
    BX1407.S66S26 2009
    242—dc22

                                                                    2009012110

Published by E.T. Nedder Publishing
An imprint of Paulist Press
997 Macarthur Blvd.
Mahwah, NJ 07430

www.paulistpress.com

Printed and bound in the
United States of America

*This book of meditations, **Desert Graces,** provides each reader with an invitation to reflect on the sacred power and the mystery of the Sonoran Desert landscape. Through a series of meditations, stillpoints, and concluding prayers, all inspired by the Sonoran Desert experience of life in and around Tucson, Arizona, the reader is gently invited to ponder the message of the prophets of long ago: "Listen to the desert and I will speak to your heart." (Hosea 2:16)*

DEDICATION

This small booklet of reflections and prayers is dedicated to the community of men and women, staff and students, who are collectively identified as the Hesychia School of Spiritual Direction.

For more information about the school and this life-giving community of men and women, representative of many diverse religious traditions, please refer to **www.desertrenewal.org**.

You are seeking for secret ways of belonging to God, but there is only one: making use of whatever God offers you.

(Jean-Pierre de Caussade)

TABLE OF CONTENTS

ORIENTATION

The Sonoran desert covers approximately 120,000 square miles primarily in southwestern Arizona, southeastern California, and the western half of the state of Sonora, Mexico. It is North America's hottest desert but also has the distinction of being the wettest desert, receiving on average anywhere from 3 to 15 inches of rain each year (depending on the specific desert location). This distinct ecosystem is home to a multitude of different species of animals including not only rattlesnakes and scorpions, which one might expect in a desert, but also bobcats, mountain lions, and numerous other mammals, birds, amphibians, and reptiles.

The Sonoran desert has the distinction of being the only place where the saguaro cactus grows naturally in the wild. In addition to the saguaro, it is also home to many plants that have evolved to have specialized adaptations to the desert climate. The Sonoran desert includes plants from the agave, palm, cactus, legume, and many other plant families.

In addition to plants, animals, and a variety of flora, the Sonoran desert is also home to 17 aboriginal American cultures including the O'odham, Ak-Chin, Gila, Salt River,

Cahuilla, Chemehuevi, Apache, Yavapai, Cocopah, Walapai, Havasupai, Clarkdale, and Prescott Yavapai Indian Communities. The spirituality of these ancient peoples continues to be preserved, nourishing and animating thriving desert communities.

Modern communities of people have also migrated to the desert and the large cities of Phoenix, Arizona (4 million), Tucson, Arizona (1 million), Mexicali, Mexico, and Hermosillo, Sonora, Mexico (900,000), and today are part of the daily rhythm and life, weaving into the fabric of the desert their stories, their personal sense of the mysterious and of the sacred.

The finest quality of this stone, these plants and animals, this desert landscape is the indifference manifest to our presence, our absence, our coming, our staying or our going. Whether we live or die is a matter of absolutely no concern whatsoever to the desert. (Edward Abbey)[1]

Treat the earth well.
It was not given to you by your parents,
it was loaned to you by your children.
We do not inherit the Earth from our Ancestors,
we borrow it from our Children.
(Ancient Indian Proverb)

---

[1] Edward Abbey, *Desert Solitaire: A Season in the Wilderness,* McGraw-Hill Book Company (New York, New York, 1968), page 267.

Introduction

The Sonoran desert is a place of destination.

People from all over the United States and Canada, and
for that matter all over the world, wind their way to this
sprawling desert oasis. Some come in search of the perfect
mineral and gem while others seek sanctuary from the cold
and the snow. Some come to be prodded, pulled, and shaped
at one of the world-class spas. Some come to be detoxed,
relaxed, and refocused in search of the same cure that their
favorite celebrity experienced. Some come seeking tickets to a
baseball spring-training game. Still others come to enjoy the
sun and perhaps a few rounds of golf. Some come to explore
and marvel at the ancient ruins left behind, many times for
no apparent reason, by the original aboriginal peoples.

With a long list of possible destinations and activities that
are trumpeted by the various tourist agencies and business
chambers, on both sides of the United States and Mexico
borders, there is at least one impetus for travel that seems
not to be at the top of the list. Perhaps it is an oversight or
perhaps it is not fully appreciated.

Relatively few people come to the desert for the stated purpose of searching for their spiritual self, but despite the lack of marketing and promotional efforts, the number of people who choose to make this distinct pilgrimage seems to be growing. It is not perhaps an accident, when all is said and done. People who travel to the desert for a spiritual purpose, and resist the tug and pull of the many other offerings of resort and shopping center, learn a valuable lesson. There is a sacredness about the desert landscape and a certain spiritual solace that can be found in the unobstructed view. With little effort a person can experience a special inner peace, a refreshment for the soul, which stands in stark contrast to the routine of everyday living.

Journeys that are pursued for a spiritual purpose have always been popular. Many of the traditional spiritualities of our human experience have a desert component as an essential ingredient in the quest for healing and wholeness. Prophets, the ancestors of the faith story of Jew, Muslim, and Christian, and even those who are known to us as our spiritual elders, the desert fathers and mothers, all knew and experienced the power of the desert. There is a special experience of the presence of God that can be encountered, and in the encounter, a person may well experience a profound moment of healing grace.

Those who take the time to journey to the desert, people who expend valuable time and resource to enjoy a few days away from their normal lives, seem to profit most from the experience. On the other hand, there are also millions of people who live here in the desert day after day — we may have to work a little harder to experience the desert as a powerful component of our spiritual personhood. Because residents have not necessarily embarked on a special journey to be here does not mean that we cannot enjoy the benefits and learn the spiritual lessons of the sacred landscape.

Residents of the Sonoran desert can be spiritually impacted day in and day out, but it will take some effort. It is not that we are not capable of the spiritual experience but rather that we may well be too familiar with the setting. The familiarity that we have with the desert does not breed contempt, but it can lull us into a sense of distraction, a take-it-for-granted attitude. We do not need to be satisfied with this response. Opportunities abound to adjust our perception and enter fully into the experience that unfolds before us.

A spiritual lesson of the desert, for both resident and visitor, teaches a person that vulnerability and patience are required in order to prosper. It does little good to be impatient or cross. Nothing is gained if a person shouts in anger or disappointment. Stomping our feet or demanding attention does not make anything move or progress at a faster pace.

These are lessons that all people know to be true, and it does not do any harm to remind ourselves of their importance.

Each unfamiliar out-of-state license plate provides an invitation to change our perception. The time we spend in each long line, waiting in anticipation for the hard-to-acquire table for dinner, is yet another opportunity. Each traffic light that seems to be longer than expected or remembered might also present a moment for necessary reflection. Each of these experiences can provide us with the opportunity to resist a growing feeling of impatience and frustration and seek rather the feeling and the emotion that leads to the fullness of life.

The spiritual pilgrims who come from near and far are often motivated to attitudinal change by the new landscape that meets their eye. If visitors can be so challenged, so too can those who are privileged to call this desert home. The grandeur of the Saguaro cactus invites reflection. The vast blue sky reminds all people of the grandeur and the splendor of the God who designs and creates. Even the very familiar prickly pear that seems to grow in every nook and cranny can be a spiritual reminder.

The winter visitor is perhaps better prepared to be surprised and to learn; it is an expectation of the journey. However, for those of us who are familiar with the desert landscape that surrounds us daily, a little extra attention to detail is important. The desert is full of grace; we just need to open our eyes and learn to appreciate what surrounds us.

STILLPOINT

The further you go into the desert, the closer you come to God. (Arabic proverb)

The bible abounds in references to the desert and the wilderness. Encounters with God, both directly and through prophetic voices, took place in scenes of desolation. God spoke on an empty stage, knowing how easily the sound of rivers diverted human attention. (Yi-Fu Tuan)[2]

All things speak of God to those who know Him, and because they reveal Him to all those who love Him, these same things hide Him from those who do not know Him. (Blaise Pascal)

"Go outside and stand on the mountain before the Lord; the Lord will be passing by." A strong and heavy wind was rending the mountains and crushing rocks before the Lord — but the Lord was not in the wind. After the wind there was an earthquake — but the Lord was not in the earthquake. After the earthquake there was fire — but the Lord was not in the

---

[2] Yi-Fu Tuan, "Attitudes toward Environment: Themes and approaches," in *Environmental Perception and Behavior,* editor David Lowenthal (Chicago, University of Chicago, 1967), page 11.

fire. After the fire there was a tiny whispering sound. When he heard this, Elijah hid his face in his cloak and went and stood at the entrance of the cave." (I Kgs 19:11-13)

SUGGESTED METHODOLGY

When you read and reflect upon the meditations that are provided in this text, it may be a good idea to use a methodology in your reflection that has been proven to be highly effective and worthwhile. Meditations can be inspiring and enjoyed without any particular methodology at work. However, meditations can also be even more profitably experienced with just a slight bit more effort.

I would suggest the following methodology to be particularly effective and worthwhile.

1. Choose a quiet place and a quiet time of the day for your meditation and reflection. Seek out perhaps a favorite chair, a particular space that you have previously enjoyed as a place where nourishment of the spirit is possible.

2. Permit yourself to become relaxed. Check the tension points on your body and make sure that there is nothing that is poking you or prodding you. Try and eliminate as many potential distractions as possible.

3. Take some deep breaths. Breathe in whatever grace you might need that will permit you to feel connected to the spirit of prayer and reflection. Try to exhale with each breath whatever it might be that is making you tense, anxious, frustrated, or distracted. Give yourself permission to let go of the troubles of the day, at least for a few precious moments.

4. Read the selected meditation from start to finish (the meditations are not strictly arranged, so feel free to pick and choose). The purpose of this first reading of the text is to become aware of the structure of the piece, the main points of reflection that are considered.

5. When you have finished reading the text, take a few moments to be present to what you have read. Try not to force a question or grab on to a point of reflection, just permit the text to be what it is.

6. After a few moments, read the text a second time and with this reading pause and reflect on any word, idea, and/or question that you might find yourself drawn to. Stay with whatever it is that focused your attention for as long as it continues to draw you. When you are ready to continue reading, return to the text again and pause only if you feel invited by the text to do so.

7. Lay the text aside and reflect on what you experienced. If you feel that the text has presented you with enough content for your reflection and perhaps prayer, then by all means enjoy the moment. If you feel that you might need a little help or direction, then read one or the other of the stillpoint quotations that are provided.

8. When you sense that the time that you have set aside for meditation and reflection is over, take one more moment and determine if there is a particular feeling, idea, challenge, or even resolution that you might want to take with you for the rest of the day as a source of nourishment and grace.

9. End your session by praying a familiar prayer or perhaps silently singing to yourself a favorite song that has been a previous source of inspiration and peace for you. If you prefer, you may choose to pray the concluding prayer that is offered in the text for your consideration.

ORDINARY PEOPLE AND ORDINARY TIME

Even the casual reader of the Jewish scriptures or the Christian Old Testament is familiar with the stories of the men and women who believers and non-believers alike identify as the ancestors in faith. Most people are familiar with the Patriarch Abraham and his invitation to be in covenant with the Lord (Gen 15). Most are also familiar with the story of Sarah who is gifted with fertility and the birth of a child long past the age when such a blessing might be considered normal and/or expected (Gen 21:1-7). Still others will easily recall the story about Jacob as he wrestles with an angel and enjoys the vision of a ladder of angels going up and coming down from the heavens (Gen 32:23-31). Other great personages of the bible also emerge with their stories, including Noah, Cain and Abel, Joshua and the walls of Jericho, and the prophet Jonah and the whale, to name just a few.

When I, not unlike many other people, read and reflect on these stories, I easily sense the awe and wonder, the moments of grace that are necessarily part and parcel of the encounter with the sacred and the profound. At the same time, however, I also experience another feeling. There is often within me a kind of longing mixed with a certain kind of questioning: "why does it seem so different today?"

The men and women of the bible experienced an easy and almost effortless encounter with the divine and the sacred. They seemed never to be surprised when they encounterd God or even one of God's angels. There is almost an expectation within them that fully accepts that such encounters and experiences of God are routine. This is not to say that they do not recognize the fact that they are blessed and chosen; nothing could be further from the truth. I intend to emphasize for our reflection what seems to be an experience of God that is in stark contrast to our own experience.

For people in our day and time the experience of the sacred and the profound is not denied, but it is also not routine. We do not easily bump up against the sacred. We do not normally encounter one of God's angels. We have to seek out the holy. In contrast to the experience of the ancestors in faith, it seems that we choose to prioritize our time and portion some of it to the church, the community, and even to our own life of prayer. More often than not if we spend a restless night we are not wrestling with God but more than likely with a specific anxiety or frustration that emerges from our daily life. Unfortunately it seems that stress is often more recognizable than the sacred.

A partial truth can emerge as we meditate and pray about our relationship with God. Is it possible that perhaps what has changed in the relationship is not God but rather us? In the ordinary times of our life, have we given up the expectation that we might encounter the divine and the graced moment? Have we reached the point where we might learn to compartmentalize and organize a little more than necessary? Is it possible that we may have used some of our gifts while at the same time ignoring other gifts and in the process lost something of importance?

I do not believe that this change in our focus was deliberate. I do not believe that the men and women of the bible were any more holy than we are today. It is not because they sought to have faith and belief while we choose another path. Rather, it is something that has happened to us, not a result of a specific decision that we have made, but instead as a consequence of the accumulation of other choices and decisions that define who we are and how we are formed.

We do not routinely encounter the sacred and the divine simply because we no longer are convinced that it is possible. We have succumbed to a vision of life that suggests that there is a proper time and place for everything. Spontaneity is often mistrusted. We tend not to like to be surprised. We desire to understand the result of something before we make a commitment to proceed. Some of us have become so protected, so isolated and so sheltered, that it might seem impossible to experience anything other than that which is already present to us.

We need to refocus our attention and perhaps shift some of our priorities. If we desire to encounter the sacred and awe-inspiring presence of God, we have to put ourselves into a position where it is at least possible. Thankfully we do not have to go very far in order to encounter the possibility of a profound experience of God: the Sonoran desert provides us with all that is needed.

Take your bible. Get your lawn chair. Go out to your backyard. Go and sit on your hotel balcony. Take a flashlight so that you can read a portion of the scripture. Then shut off your light and look up into the heavens. Look at the stars. Listen to the coyotes. Feel the gentle breeze. Smell and feel the heat that surrounds you. Wait in anticipation for the lessons of the desert and you will not be disappointed.

*The most beautiful thing we can experience is the mysterious.
It is the source of all true art and science. He to whom this
emotion is a stranger, who can no longer pause to wonder
and stand rapt in awe, is as good as dead: his eyes are closed.*
(Albert Einstein)

*Earth is crammed with heaven and every common bush afire
with God: but only the man who sees takes off his shoes. The
rest sit round it and pluck blackberries.* (Elizabeth Barrett
Browning, *Aurora Leigh*)

*We are not human beings having spiritual experiences,
we are spiritual beings having human experiences.*
(Teilhard de Chardin, S.J.)

*The best remedy for those who are afraid, lonely or unhappy is
to go outside, somewhere where they can be quiet, alone with
the heavens, nature and God. Because only then does one feel
that all is as it should be and that God wishes to see people
happy, amidst the simple beauty of nature.* (Anne Frank)

CONCLUDING PRAYER

Yahweh, Elohim, al-Lah, God is the presence
in whom my being comes alive
the core and ground of my existence
the infinite and inexhaustible ground of all being
the source of life and goodness
the fountain of all holiness
the originator of unconditional love and
the initiator of the Big Bang.

This presence calls me to fullness of life
to praise and thanksgiving
to integrity and wholesomeness and
to courageous vulnerable love.

Rabbi Jesus the Messiah teaches me
to live fully
to act justly
to love tenderly
to walk humbly with my God and
where necessary to lose graciously.
(Kevin G. Smith, *In the Presence of God*)

Rekindle the Romance

In a relationship between two people, when the relationship develops into a commitment that will lead eventually to engagement and then marriage, there is often a defining experience. The experience might be as simple as a song remembered within the context of a specific event or a favorite place for dinner. Another experience, perhaps something that requires a little more effort, might be the memory of a treasured vacation, or the birth of their first child, or even as dramatic as a prolonged argument that did not end in anger but rather in the realization that "I just cannot live without you, no matter how wrong you might be!" Regardless of the form that it might take, each person understands the experience as a defining moment in the relationship. It is easily recalled years later on the occasion of an anniversary or perhaps around the dinner table in answer to the probing question of one of the children, "When did you and Mom know that you were in love?"

In any relationship, as the years go by, there are moments when the relationship is fully animated and energized. There are still other moments when there may be a struggle and some difficulty. It is not unusual, if a couple desires to ignite and to rediscover the intensity of what they experienced when the relationship was new and fresh, to recall the experience that punctuated the romance. On such an occasion they often return to the original and special defining moment remembered in an effort to breathe new life and energy into the present reality. It is a good practice to return to the special place or experience and recall how it once was so that you may believe that it can be that way again.

For the people of Israel, in the Old Testament story of the covenant between Yahweh and the people, the desert was the animating experience, the special place that the people would return to when a spark was needed in their relationship. The desert was the place where Israel, wandering for 40 years in Exodus from the captivity in Egypt, learned to first love Yahweh as their God. Up until the moment of the Exodus, the experience of the covenant between Yahweh and his people was primarily experienced through the intercession of a single person such as Abraham, Isaac, Rebecca, and Jacob. At the moment of Exodus, however, the experience became a community experience. It is not too much of an exaggeration to assert that the experience of the desert was, for the people of Israel, the beginning of their romance, the defining moment in their relationship. "When did you and Yahweh know that you were in love?"

As a result of this understanding, whenever the people of Israel suffered from a wandering eye, when they were distracted by whatever it might be that did not come from Yahweh, it was not unusual for the prophets, the messengers of God, to exhort them to remember and to recall the beginning moments of the relationship. The prophet Hosea clearly makes the connection when he tells that people to "go to the desert where I will speak to your heart." Hosea challenged the people of the covenant to rekindle the romance that they had with Yahweh by returning to the moment when the relationship was new, fresh, and full of energy. It's not unlike what a struggling couple might do when faced with the same kind of situation.

The experience of the desert has often played a central role in the spiritual journey of the people of God, including the people of the new covenant, the Kingdom of God. Again and again we read in the New Testament that Jesus would go off to a desert place, a place in the wilderness of the Holy Land, and there become refreshed and nourished through his encounter with the Father. The great saints of the first and second century, men and women that we identify today as the desert Abbas and Ammas of our spiritual heritage, repeated the example of Jesus. It would not be too much of an exaggeration to assert that the experience of the desert was, for our direct ancestors in faith, the place where they too learned to rekindle their romance with the Lord. The desert was the place where they discovered a new, fresh, and fulfilling energy.

For many people in our time and place, not just men and women long remembered but buried in the mist of centuries long past, the desert has the same power. For these people, contemporary, up-to-date, and very much tuned into the present moment, the experience that is provided by the Sonoran desert, oftentimes on their first encounter, has become a defining memory in their spiritual journey. The desert experience, recalled more often than not by specific moments that stand out as exceptional encounters with something or someone other than themselves, seems to be "hardwired" into the core of their being. The experience is easily recalled and capable of the continued and sustained nourishment of their souls for many years to come.

"When did you first know that you were in love?"

STILLPOINT

That one I love who is incapable of ill will,
who is friendly and compassionate.

Living beyond the reach of I and mine
and of pleasure and pain,
patient, contented, self-controlled,
firm in faith, with all his heart and
all his mind given to me —
with such a one I am in love.
(Bhagavad Gita 12:13-14)

To seek is as good as seeing. God wants us to search earnestly
and with perseverance, without sloth and worthless sorrow. We
must know that God will appear suddenly and joyfully to all
lovers of God. (Julian of Norwich)[3]

There comes a moment when the children who have been
playing at burglars hush suddenly: was that a real footstep in
the hall? There comes a moment when people who have been
dabbling in religion....suddenly draw back. Supposing we
really found Him? We never meant it to come to that! Worse
still, supposing He has found us?" (C. S. Lewis)[4]

We have to be in a desert. For He whom we must love is
absent...We must be rooted in the absence of a place.
(Simone Weil)

---

[3] Doyle, Brendan, *Meditations with Julian of Norwich,* Bear and
Company (Santa Fe, NM, 1986), page 36.
[4] C. S. Lewis, *Miracles,* Collins (London, 1947), page 98.

CONCLUDING PRAYER

Supreme God, your light is brighter than the sun,
your purity whiter than mountain snow, you are present
wherever I go.

All people of wisdom praise you.

So I too put faith in all your words, knowing that everything you teach is true.

Neither the angels in heaven nor the demons in hell can
know the perfection of your wisdom, for it is beyond
all understanding.

Only your Spirit knows you; only you can know
your true self.

You are the source of all being, the power of all power,
the ruler of all creatures.

So you alone understand what you are.

In your mercy reveal to me all that I need to know,
in order to find peace and joy.

Tell me the truths that are necessary for the world
in which I live.

Show me how I can meditate upon you, learning from
you the wisdom that I need.

I am never tired of hearing you, because your words
bring life.

("The Truth Of God," Bhagavad Gita)

RESPECT THE MYSTERY

We live in a culture that is very comfortable with maxims, theories, and the accumulation and interpretation of scientific data. We effortlessly maneuver through a constant stream of electronic gadgetry in which today's newest toy becomes tomorrow's necessary accessory. We acknowledge the importance of scientific experimentation and live in anticipation of the latest discovery that will enlighten and inspire us.

With very few exceptions, we are generally uncomfortable with anything that cannot be analyzed and studied. We fully believe that we are probably just one molecule away from discovering a cure for the common cold. We have certitude that the newest telescope will help us discover a new unknown galaxy or perhaps a black hole. We are confident that a powerful engine will produce the experience of "warp drive" and we will finally be able to travel easily beyond the reach of earth's gravitational pull and explore the universe that stretches out before us.

Acknowledging the giftedness and the blessings that have

been given to us by the discoveries of science, we may question our ability to acknowledge a deeper truth. Futhermore, for hundreds of millions of people who call the earth their home, all that we take for granted is unknown, unreachable, and not at all part of their lived reality and experience.

It may be hard to imagine, but there are huge populations of people for whom there is a comfort level and familiarity that is radically other than that which is powered by the scientific method. There are numerous cultures that are animated, and energized not by a maxim or a theory but rather primarily by story, custom, and ritual. The people of these different and vibrant cultures experience and interpret the world through a lens that we may not fully respect or appreciate. This does not mean that their experience is somehow not authentic, important, and even capable of inspiring great devotion and meaning.

There is a challenge and a lesson or two here that is worth learning. Perhaps in the contrast, and even in the occasional clash between two divergent experiences of life, we might glimpse something that is essential and important for us.

The first lesson that we can learn is the need to come to a deeper understanding and appreciation for the human experience of life that goes beyond our own. Not everything in life needs to be understood or explained. There is power, some would assert that there is a sacred power, in not knowing and just accepting. There is something of great value in mystery. It is worth the effort to learn to respect it.

A second lesson is also important to recall. To embrace and acknowledge the power and the sacredness of mystery is not to deny the power and the importance of that which can be studied and documented. The scientific method and all that it has blessed us with is not the enemy of mystery or of the sacred. At the same time, however, we must also acknowledge that faith and belief will at times not sufficiently inform or enlighten the human spirit. We are capable of discovery and learning just as we are capable of believing and accepting.

The desert can once again teach us a valuable lesson and provide a helpful perspective. The experience of the early dawn in the Sonoran desert can be very enlightening and potentially integrating.

Knowing the intricacies of how the colors of the morning sky are formed does not take away from the power of the experience. Understanding how the crispness of the morning air is calculated in Fahrenheit and Celsius does not mean that the light morning jacket can be left hanging in the closet because you will be somehow warmed by the knowledge of measurement. Determining to open up the palms of your hands, stretching them toward the heavens in anticipation of God's abundant grace does not indicate a disrespect for what can be measured and analyzed. Praying a prayer of thanksgiving and blessing does not somehow make you less intelligent or curious.

The desert teaches a powerful lesson if we are only open to receiving it. It is not necessary to define the gift of life that we have been blessed with as either/or. There is a power in the both/and.

I believe in the necessity of probing, testing, measuring, and then defining, proposing, and then repeating the method until a particular result emerges. I also believe in silence, anticipation, and patiently waiting until that which needs to be revealed has been gifted to me. I don't expect my science to explain my faith, and I do not fear that my faith will somehow be taken away by my science. I hope that I have learned to respect the mystery of science, faith, and desert.

STILLPOINT

I accept Reality and dare not question it,
Materialism first and last imbuing.
Hurrah for positive science! long live exact demonstration!
Fetch stonecrop mixt with cedar and branches of lilac,
This is the lexicographer, this the chemist, this made a

grammar of the old cartouches,
These mariners put the ship through dangerous unknown seas.
This is the geologist, this works with the scalper, and this is
a mathematician.

Gentlemen, to you the first honors always!
Your facts are useful, and yet they are not my dwelling,
I but enter by them to an area of my dwelling.
(Walt Whitman, *Song of Myself*)

You know that I like all that I am hearing.
You know that I find the world too busy.
My life is too busy.
Everything geared toward success, and away from you.
You know that I'm resonating with everything that
I am hearing.
Please, God…once I am back home:
Don't let me forget. (Jeannette Angell)[5]

---

[5] Angell, Jeannette L., *All Ground is Holy, A Guide to the Christian Retreat,* Morehouse Publishing (Harrisburg, PA, 1993), page 62.

CONCLUDING PRAYER

Great Spirit, God, Creator of All
I welcome You into my heart, mind, body and soul
There is always room for You here.
Grant me the wisdom to heed my inner voice
And the strength to stay grounded while I sing
my sacred song.
Guide me down my chosen path and give me the
courage to pursue what is available to me.
I am thankful for the lessons and grateful for
my struggles;
I have not forgotten what has brought me to
where I am today.
Open my heart to the healing wholeness of nature;
We are all related, and through this I will find serenity.
Great Spirit, God, Creator of All
Cleanse my spirit and wash my soul.
There is always room for You here.

(Laurel Singing Water Cat)

Essential Nourishment

The desert has a way of bringing a person face to face with one experience, and then a moment or two later, the flip side of the same experience.

The brilliant skies give way — it seems almost in an instant — to complete darkness. The warmth of the day is loosened and gives way to a penetrating cold. The hustle and the bustle of activity, and the routine sounds that punctuate the normal comings and goings of the day, are quieted as the day draws to a close. First one, and then the other, is the normal rhythm of the desert, the animating spirit and energy of this sacred landscape.

In the midst of this daily concert of the creative power of God there is one experience that should not be ignored, neglected, or passed without some kind of focused reflection. Perhaps late at night or very early in the morning, depending on the perception of the individual, the desert sojourner is invited to become attentive to the presence of a very important experience. Each day we are routinely treated to one of God's awesome gifts of love, but we need to develop an awareness of the gift lest it pass us by.

The gift is silence, the flip side of noise, distraction, and business as usual. Just as assuredly as sun gives way to darkness, and heat gives way to cold, frantic activity daily gives way, at least for a moment, to the possibility of silence. It is an experience that is offered to us and we are invited to partake of the nourishment that it gives.

It may seem somewhat startling to imagine silence as a gift of God's love. It may seem somewhat difficult to understand silence as a type of nourishment but, in effect, that is what silence is for each spiritual traveler, each human person.

Just as water is required by the desert to nourish and grow all that lives here, so is silence required by the soul. Just as food is required, and some foods are craved by the human person, so is silence required by the soul. Just as oxygen is required in order to breathe and to live, so is silence required by the soul. Silence is the essential nourishment of the soul and to deprive the soul of this essential nutrient is to deprive it of life.

Any spiritual practice, no matter how sincere a person might be, no matter how committed a person may be to the discipline required, will eventually die without silence because it is not nourished. A spiritual practice without silence is like the seed that is sown "on rocky ground, where it has little soil....since the soil had no depth...it began to wither for lack of roots." (Mt. 13:5)

Silence provides nourishment.
Silence promotes spiritual growth.
Silence allows for the spiritual practice to take root.

If a person has a decision to make, a choice necessitated by the other demands and requirements of their life, between silence and any other spiritual practice, the choice should be for the experience of silence. Everything else will eventually catch up and work itself out. Silence cannot be replaced with activity, with learning, with good intentions, with ritual or with any other experience. It is that important.

Fortunately, the desert provides each seeker of spiritual nourishment with the ever-present invitation to partake of the silence that is necessary. There are many moments of potential silence in the day, from the ordinary to the extraordinary, from the common to the dramatic, that may be encountered without much effort on our part.

Ordinary moments can be as simple as the choice not to turn on the car radio as a person is stuck in traffic or as the morning commute is engaged. Still other moments are provided by choosing to lie quietly in bed for a few extra minutes before beginning the routine of the day. Pacing ourselves throughout the day to provide opportunities when we can transverse from one task to another, to reflect on what we have completed and to ponder what lies ahead, can be another example of a nourishing period of silence.

More sustained silence, that can provide the possibility of the extraordinary and dramatic experience of grace, might take a little more planning.

A hike to a favorite desert vantage point, a little off the beaten track, is often a powerful experience of silence. Picking up your favorite lawn chair, moving it into the center of your backyard, staking out a private spot on the grounds of the resort that you are visiting, enjoying the warm embrace of the cosmic universe around you, can be an experience of silence and contemplation that is unsurpassed. A visit to enjoy the abiding presence of God in any of our churches, mosques, or synagogues can also be powerfully nourishing and fulfilling.

Listen to the desert, and in the listening you will encounter the power and the grace of the essential nutrient of the soul, the gift of silence.

*Whenever there is some silence around you — listen to it.
That means just notice it. Pay attention to it. Listening to
silence awakens the dimension of stillness within yourself,
because it is only through stillness that you can be aware of
silence.* (Eckhart Tolle)[6]

*When the Lord wishes to draw a soul to himself, he leads it
into solitude, far from the embarrassment of the world and
intercourse with men, and there speaks to it with words of
fire. The words of God are said to be of fire, because they melt
a soul...In fact, they prepare the soul to submit readily to the
direction of God.* (St. Alphonsus Liguori, C.Ss.R.)

*Before you speak, it is necessary for you to listen,
for God speaks in the silence of the heart.* (Mother Teresa)

*It is of the greatest importance to practice a regular period
of withdrawal. When a person does not reflect on the real
purpose of his life, what meaning is there to his existence?*
(Nahman of Bratslav)

---

[6] Tolle, Eckhart, *Stillness Speaks,* Namaste Publishers (Vancouver,
Canada), page 4.

O GREAT SPIRIT
help me always
to speak the truth quietly,
to listen with an open mind
when others speak,
and to remember the peace
that may be found in silence.
(Cherokee Prayer)

CONCLUDING PRAYER

To the divine silence of unreachable endlessness;

To the divine silence of perfected knowledge;

To the divine silence of the soundless voice;

To the divine silence of the Heart of the Labyrinth;

To the divine silence of the ancient mind;

To the divine silence of the unborn guide;

To the divine silence of the unseen guide,

protector of all sentient life;

To the divine silence of those of perfected knowledge;

To the divine silence of human primate incarnation;

To the divine silence of the labyrinth guides

who sacrifice their liberation for those

who have not yet awakened to the truth;

To the divine silence of the Lord of Death,

the eternal unborn resident of the labyrinth

who has sacrificed his own redemption

for the redemption of all voyagers everywhere;

To the divine silence of the primordial being;

To the divine silence of the great sacrifice;

We offer homage, love and hope;

But above all, we give our gratitude.

(E. J. Gold, *American Book of the Dead*)

Hug Me!

I have a friend who often observes, "There is nothing in the desert that says 'hug me.'" His observation is rooted in his perception that seemingly every cactus, and even other desert flora, all have some sort of pricker system that protects them from natural predators. This system of barbs and thorns works well; if a person has an unexpected encounter with any of these protected desert cacti more often than not it is the human person who comes out the loser. As a result of the encounter you can be sure that you will devote the next few minutes, and sometimes even longer than a few minutes, to trying to extract from your body what the cactus has attached to a finger, the side of the arm, or an unprotected area of the leg.

The desert's non-huggable cacti and other flora can serve as a kind of metaphor for reflection and meditation. As we perceive and experience the cacti, so too can the human person sometimes be both perceived and experienced.

There are people, whom we encounter in our daily experience of life, who seem to have nothing about them that says

"Hug me." Not unlike the desert cacti that are able to repel the perceived predator, they too are seemingly able to "repel" people who desire to encounter them. Instead of a welcoming smile you encounter rather the frown or the scowl. Instead of a cheerful "hello," the experience is a grunt or a less-than-enthusiastic greeting of some kind. On the occasion where you might nevertheless persist in your desire to engage such a person, despite their defense system, you can easily spend the next few minutes and sometimes even longer wondering what happened when your encounter turns out to be less than what you might have imagined. The experience can often be just as unpleasant as removing the barb from a cactus that sticks in your finger.

Is it possible to hug a cactus or a person who seems to not want to be hugged? Again, the desert can teach us a valuable lesson.

Observe the cactus very closely, even the ones that seem to be covered with prickers and barbs, such as the cholla cactus. In the midst of the branches of this splendid cactus it would not be unusual to discover a nesting place for the desert wren. The nest is completely surrounded by the repelling barbs, but somehow the wren is able to penetrate the barbs and construct a nest. The barbs that seem to repel become a web of protection for the wren and the eggs and young birds that will soon arrive. The wren knows how to avoid the barbs and is not discouraged by what seems to be an overwhelming obstacle. The cactus might not be "hugging" the wren, but it nevertheless partners with the wren to provide a place of safety and security for the task of parenting.

The cooperative relationship between the cholla cactus and the desert wren can be the model of what may also be accomplished with the human person who seems to repel rather than attract other people. Perhaps what is necessary to learn is the approach to friendship and relationship that seems safe and which will be welcomed rather than an approach that causes fear and anxiety and the automatic response that pushes away instead of welcomes. It might also be necessary to remind ourselves that the person who might be sending off the strongest aura of a non-welcoming presence might very well be the person who needs to be hugged the most.

Is it worth the effort? Imagine how surprised and pleased you might be when you discover and experience the desert wren secured and safe in her nest in the foreboding cholla. Don't you find yourself marveling at what looks like a small miracle? So too the same kind of experience and sense of wonder and awe when the person that you encounter and perceive, who was once so different, aloof, and seemingly not worth the effort, springs forth into life and reveals to you the miracle of what happens when they encounter persistent love, despite the obstacle and the challenge.

We might want to be careful what we choose to hug when we walk through the desert. On the other hand we might choose to not be so picky or easily discouraged, despite the perceived obstacle, when we encounter another human person who could use a hug, a gentle word, or just an accepting and cheerful smile.

STILLPOINT

Thousands of candles can be lighted from a single candle,
and the life of the candle will not be shortened.
Happiness never decreases by being shared. (Buddha)

It is not how much we do,
but how much love we put in the doing.
It is not how much we give,
but how much love we put in the giving. (Mother Teresa)

"Encouragement is oxygen to the soul." (Harvey Mackay)

If you treat people the way they are, you make them worse.
If you treat them the way they ought to be, you make
them capable of becoming what they ought to be.
(Johann Wolfgang von Goethe)

CONCLUDING PRAYER

I behold the Christ in you.

I place you lovingly in the care of the All Caring One.

I release you from my anxiety and concern.

I let go of my possessive hold on you.

I am willing to free you to follow the dictates of

the indwelling Spirit.

I am willing to free you to live your life

      according to your best light and understanding.

Husband, wife, child, friend,

I no longer try to force my ideas on you, my ways on you.

I lift my thoughts above you, above the personal level.

I see you as God sees you,

a spiritual being,

created in God's image,

endowed with qualities and abilities that

make you needed

      and important not only to me but to God and

God's larger perspective.

I do not bind you.

I no longer believe that you do not have

the understanding you need in order to meet life.

I bless you

I have faith in you,

I behold Jesus in you. *(Herve Marcoux, OMI)*

Wake Up!

"Spirituality," according to the Jesuit retreat director and spiritual writer Father Anthony DeMello, "means waking up." Developing a spiritual awareness and a focus requires discipline and practice; surprisingly we are not automatically "awake" in the spiritual sense. This lesson needs to be learned and the Sonoran desert can be one of our best teachers.

I begin most of my days early in the morning walking through the desert on my way to the place where I routinely join with a community of men and women who meet for contemplative prayer. This early morning walk is different during the seasons of the year. In the summer months it is already bright, clear, hot, and dry. In the winter months it is cold, sometimes bordering on the freezing, and the stars and planets still shine bright as they wait for the morning sun to appear.

One recent morning with the normal desert sounds, views, and smells filling my senses, a remote preparation for the meditation and prayer that was soon to come, the desert reached out to me and invited me to an experience of awakening. The desert challenged me to "wake-up" and to experience something that seemed at first glance to be ordinary but which was in reality truly extraordinary.

I found my attention focused on a simple piece of wood wedged in between two slabs of cement, I suppose to provide the necessary space for the expansion and the contraction of the sidewalk. That may well have been the intent of the original contractor, but the desert had another idea. When I looked closely at the piece of wood I noticed something entirely different. What slowly came into view was in fact a desert highway, a busy interstate as busy as Interstate 10 or 19, for a colony of ants.

The ants were passing each other with great furor, coming and going, back and forth on this piece of wood. Seemingly, much to my amazement, all were aware of the rules that governed the use of this desert highway since there never seemed to be any kind of disruption in the flow. As I focused my attention even more on the display unfolding before me I would notice the occasional ant attempting to pull a piece of food along the highway. I imagined the ant to be some sort of interstate trucker, an important cog in the transport and the supply of the colony. However most of the ants seemed only to be busily intent on their business, and going to and from a place of obvious importance.

I wondered, on this beautiful desert morning, if it would be possible to stop one of these busy ants in its frantic comings and goings? I wondered if it would be possible to interrupt the flow and routine and "interview" one of the ants? I imagined that the story an ant might share would be riveting. Undoubtedly the story would be filled with the trials and the tribulations, the joys and the challenges of the ant colony. If, after a few minutes of listening to the story, I might dare to probe a little more, I wonder if this busy ant could tell me anything of the world that surrounds the colony? I wonder, for example, if the ant is aware of the fact that just a few short feet away there is another piece of wood, not unlike the busy desert highway the ants travel each day, but seemingly not used and quite abandoned. Does it not go to a necessary place? Is there something different about this piece of wood that I do not understand or appreciate? Are only certain special ants invited to journey in this space and then only on special occasions? Is it just the familiar story of location, location?

If I had the courage to probe even deeper I wonder if this ant could share with me thoughts about some kind of higher ant or perhaps even God; I wonder if ants even have those kinds of thoughts? Would I hear in response to my question a wonderful mythic story, detailing the story of the ancestor ants who had gone before, or would the ant know nothing of why he/she was present this day, on this particular desert highway, answering my probing questions?

I permitted myself to imagine for a few more moments the possible meaning of what unfolded before me, but then I caught myself and corrected my course. I reminded myself that this was no highway but rather a little piece of wood, in the middle of the desert, making sure that the cement remained strong. I suppose a person would be foolish to make too much out of it, and so I straightened myself out, stretched and yawned, and continued on my way to the waiting community, in order to pray and to meditate about God.

STILLPOINT

Words can enhance experience, but they can also take so much away. We see an insect and at once we abstract certain characteristics and classify it — a fly. And in that very cognitive exercise, part of the wonder is gone. Once we have labeled the things around us we do not bother to look at them so carefully. Words are part of our rational selves, and to abandon them for a while is to give freer reign to our intuitive selves.
(Jane Goodall, *Reason for Hope*)

Love the animals, love the plants, love everything. If you love everything, you will perceive the divine mystery in things. Once you perceive it, you will begin to comprehend it better every day. And you will come at last to love the whole world with an all-embracing love. (Fyodor Dostoyevsky)

People usually consider walking on water or in thin air a miracle. But I think the real miracle is not to walk either on water or in thin air, but to walk on earth. Every day we are engaged in a miracle which we don't even recognize: a blue sky, white clouds, green leaves, the black, curious eyes of a child —our own two eyes. All is a miracle. (Thich Nhat Hanh)

CONCLUDING PRAYER

Creator hear us, for we are your children.
Father we thank you for all that you have given us.
We thank you for the lessons that you have taught us and
for the life that you have allowed us to lead.
We thank you Mother Earth for your beauty
and sustenance.
We thank the masters of this universe
for their guidance, protection and direction.
Father we thank you for the white light that surrounds us,
and for that same white light which transmutes
all negativity into love and healing.

We thank you father, for the healing of our souls,
the healing of the Earth and for the healing of
all mankind.
We call upon the power of the universe, to
allow us happiness, prosperity, healing and love.
We call upon the power of the universe for
good relationship to all things.
We call upon the power of the universe, for
sacred direction,
sacred protection, sacred correction and
sacred connection.
We call upon the power of the universe for
magic and miracles.
We honor you Creator, as we honor all things
seen and unseen.
We honor you Creator, as we honor our ancestors,
as we honor ourselves.

(Grant Redhawk-Two Feathers)

SACRED INTIMACY

Looming before us, at a day and an hour not of our own
choosing, is a personal and intimate encounter with our God.
This encounter is inescapable, beyond our control or decision.
It is the necessary outcome of the linking together that
occurred in the biological dance of life at the moment
of our creation.

Despite our best efforts and our ability to oftentimes deny
what has been chosen for us, the encounter will take place.

It is a personal encounter for which there is no substitution
possible. We cannot plead, whine, buy, or bluff our way
out of it.

It is an encounter with God in whatever form we imagine
God to be. It is not dependent on our distractive desire
to name, dogmatize, appease, or ignore. It simply and
profoundly is.

"Do not let your hearts be troubled" (John 14:27).

Despite the fact that this encounter is inescapable, it should
not be a source of anxiety, frustration, or even dread.

It is not the experience of being disciplined by a parent.
It is not a trip to the principal's office.
It is not being summoned before your superiors and the
review board for a performance evaluation.

Perhaps, somewhere in your experience of life, oftentimes
within the context of what you might understand as religious
life and practice, you have undoubtedly encountered another
who has attempted to convince you otherwise. Their effort
may well be sincere, but it is misplaced.

Sacred intimacy trumps anxiety.
Sacred intimacy trumps fear.
Sacred intimacy trumps imaginings.

Each created person will one day be invited into this intimate
encounter, the most intimate encounter possible. It is an
encounter with the only Other who knows and loves you
completely, exactly as you are, not as you might one day be,
and even perhaps have struggled to become.

There are no secrets.
There is nothing that can be hidden.
All is exposed to the light.

In this encounter there is authentic and complete intimacy,
and intimacy that is ultimately sacred. In fact, unknown to

you except in the deepest and truest part of yourself, you have been waiting for this moment for a lifetime.

It is not required that you anticipate the moment that is to come.
It is not required that you accept what cannot be changed.

The desert teaches a lesson even here. The seemingly terrifying vulnerability of being planted and secured in place, not unlike the saguaro and ocotillo, provides the focus point.

A cactus cannot will it otherwise. A cactus cannot brush away the desert wren who seeks to build a nest. A cactus cannot seek the shade of the palo verde to escape the desert heat. A cactus cannot seek protective shelter in the middle of an electric storm or the monsoon downpour.

We are not unlike the desert cacti. We sometimes perceive that we are ultimately in control of our lives, but it is the ultimate illusion. We are tethered, we are planted, and we are not the gardener who is in charge of the transplanting.

Long ago the cacti of the desert learned the lesson of letting go and letting God, which fuels the experience of acceptance and not of struggle. With the grace of acceptance, perhaps, the ultimately fulfilling experience of majestic glory is anticipated and even celebrated.

It is a lesson well worth learning.

It is a truth well worth practicing.

STILLPOINT

*In every movement God is present since it is impossible to make
any move or utter a word without the might of God.* (Dov Baer
of Mexhirich)

The only thing that burns in hell
is the part of you that won't let go of your life:
your memories, your attachments.
They burn them all away, but they're not punishing you,
they're freeing your soul.
If you're frightened of dying and you're holding on,
you'll see devils tearing your life away.
If you've made your peace,
then the devils are really angels freeing you from the earth.
(Meister Eckhart)

CONCLUDING PRAYER
My Lord God, I have no idea where I am going.

I do not see the road ahead of me.

I cannot know for certain where it will end.

Nor do I really know myself,
  and the fact that I think that I am following your will
  does not mean that I am actually doing so.
But I believe that the desire to please you does in fact
  please you.
And I hope that I have that desire in all that I am doing.
I hope that I will never do anything apart from
  that desire.
And I know that if I do this you will lead me
  by the right road though I may know nothing about it.
Therefore I will trust you always
  though I may seem to be lost and in the
  shadow of death.
I will not fear, for you are ever with me,
  and will never leave me to face my perils alone.
(Thomas Merton)

The Lesson of the Saguaro

A necessary and important if not essential skill for the spiritual journey is to learn to be patient. Very quickly we learn as we begin the journey that "God's ways are not our ways," and "that a thousand years are like a day in the eyes of the Lord." No experience brings this truth into clearer focus than the time we might spend in prayer.

Prayer requires a commitment. The relationship between the individual person and the God who has called him/her to the sacred experience of prayer cannot be rushed. There are no shortcuts. There are no credible methods that can be engaged or practiced that will bypass the requirement for patience. All the great saints preach this truth. All the great mystics require that the truth be accepted and embraced. Whether Catholic, Protestant, Jew, or Moslem, believer or unbeliever, the requirement does not change.

Learn the importance of this lesson if not from the saints and the mystics, then from the majestic saguaro cactus. The saguaro, unique to our Sonoran desert, surrounds us and dots the landscape. The saguaro seems always to be positioned in our line of sight, perhaps inviting us to encounter an important truth.

The saguaro stands and patiently waits. Straight and tall. Narrow and bent. Five arms or 10 arms. It seems not to matter. Each saguaro, no matter how it might look, no matter where it might be rooted, is invited to respond by its Creator God to the sun, the heat and the cold, the monsoon wind and rain, in exactly the same way. Ten years, 30 years, 50 years, even 200 years—the lesson is learned, repeated, and learned again. Patience.

We can become challenged daily to look at the saguaro and see in this gift from God a constant reminder of what is required of us. Despite our inclination to distraction, despite our ability to confuse ourselves with too many questions or with an impatience for results, we are invited to learn, accept, and embrace the truth that all will be accomplished in God's time. We cannot rush God's plan. We cannot speed up what we think needs to be accomplished. We cannot bargain for a better result. We cannot insist on our own opinion or judgment. The saguaro teaches us to be patient, to learn the lesson, to repeat it, and to learn it again.

The saguaro teaches the willing student 24/7, but perhaps the lesson is most profound at sunset. When we take the time and turn our vision to the west, we stand with the saguaro. If we too have the courage to lift our hands in prayer, opening them and letting go of all that we think we need, we can assume the sacred position, the position that teaches us to be patient, to wait in eager anticipation for whatever it might be that the Lord determines we need.

There is a special power that happens when a person stands before God like the saguaro in supplication, with hands wide open. It is in the gesture itself, a gesture that admits helplessness and invites the strength of another, that we are best able to experience the presence of the God who calls. Again, it doesn't happen all at once. The experience is powerful in the silence and the gentleness of the moment. It cannot be managed, administered, toggled, or adjusted in any manner or form other than what it is. Patience. Learn the lesson of patience, and then repeat it, again and again.

STILLPOINT

God is ready to give great things when we are ready...to give up everything. (Meister Eckhart)

"Every authentic religious epiphany or encounter, every true experience of God, in whatever form, makes a person less insular, less complacent, and less isolated—and more restless, more inspired and more engaged with the world and humanity." (Anthony Gittins)[7]

Being . . .
It is the letting go of all the
should's, the must's, the have-to's,
the have-nots, the cannots,
the doubts and the guilt.
It is allowing your thoughts to come forth -
without judgment.
It is allowing yourself to feel -
without judgment.
It is allowing yourself to do what you want -
without judgment.
It is allowing yourself to be who you are -
without judgment.
When you allow yourself to be,
You find
Peace, Freedom, Love and Joy
Within you. (Author Unknown)

---

[7] *A Presence That Disturbs: A Call to Radical Discipleship,* Anthony J. Gittins, Liguori/Triumph (Liguori, Missouri, 2002), page 12.

CONCLUDING PRAYER

We return thanks to our mother, the earth,

which sustains us.

We return thanks to the rivers and streams,

which supply us with water.

We return thanks to all herbs,

which furnish medicines for the cure of our diseases.

We return thanks to the moon and stars,

which have given to us their light when the sun was gone.

We return thanks to the sun,

that has looked upon the earth with a beneficent eye.

Lastly, we return thanks to the Great Spirit,

in Whom is embodied all goodness,

and Who directs all things for the good of Her children.

(Iroquois Prayer)

GENTLE ARMS LIFTED UP

The mighty saguaro cactus, the state flower of Arizona, invariably captivates the imagination and focus of many visitors to our Sonoran desert. There is a certain grandeur and mystery about this distinctive cactus that invites comment, reflection, and then ultimately a barrage of questions. The most common question asked by the inquiring guest seems to be in reference to the presence of the many and varied branches or arms of the saguaro. When it is patiently explained that the saguaro must be approximately 75 years old before the first arm appears and gently curves upward, there is a reaction of surprise. "Then, how old are the saguaros?" can often be a follow-up question to the initial inquiry. When it is explained that a typical saguaro (if there is such a creature) is 30 feet tall, has five arms and is approximately 200 years old, even more wonderment is expressed.

Upon reflection, even with the data provided by scientific observation, it is a difficult exercise to imagine that the saguaro is routinely 75 years old before the first arm begins to grow. A possible source of this difficulty might be discovered when we examine a perception that we hold that animates our sense of wonder. Many people seem to believe that 75 years old is not the age when we should expect, or for that matter even encourage, any type of growth or development. However what seems to be the practice among some human beings evidently is not the practice in the world of cacti: the saguaro confronts our limited perception and challenges us to understand and perceive reality in a different manner. There is also a profound spiritual truth at work here that we might profit from.

"To see in a different way," to perceive reality from the beginning standpoint of the Kingdom of God, is essential to understanding the life and ministry of Jesus. Again and again the Lord confronted and confounded his listeners with a certain truth that seemed to fly in the face of what was commonly accepted. Often Jesus presented a challenge that would certainly be more profound than even that modeled by the saguaro and its pattern of growth.

"Look at the birds in the air, they neither sow or reap but your heavenly Father feeds them" (Mt 6:26). Or in another place, "Martha, Martha, you are worried and distracted by many things; there is need of only one thing. Mary has chosen the better part, which will not be taken away from her" (Lk 10:41-42). Or even in answer to what seemed to be an insignificant question, "For those who want to save their life will lose it, and those who lose their life for my sake will save it" (Lk 9:24). In each instance, and in many other places and encounters, Jesus illustrated through his life and witness the importance of not seeing what seemed to be so obvious but rather to make the effort and try to see as God might see.

When we attempt to perceive life from the perspective offered to us by the Kingdom of God, the saguaro's 75-year-old growth spurt is not as surprising. We recognize the power of grace at work in our lives and assume that this grace is abundant, never tires, and is certainly not in short supply. Just as a saguaro begins to grow a new arm, so too do our brothers and sisters continue to grow and develop, each day learning more and more to see as God sees. There is no age barrier to the power of grace. At times we are even able to recognize that the accumulation of years and the experiences that define each day of life are in fact necessary to truly understand and fully appreciate a specific truth. Hopefully, when we reflect on our life, we will notice that the passing of the years has softened our opinions and judgments and made us more aware of the possibilities rather than just the difficulties of life.

Permit the gently lifted arms of the old and wise saguaro to teach you a lesson about the power of grace at work in your life. Expect that you will be blessed and gifted this day, regardless of your age, and try to see in the witness of the desert an invitation to see something of the presence of the Kingdom of God at work all around you.

STILLPOINT

"There is nothing that wastes the body like worry, and one who has any faith in God should be ashamed to worry about anything whatsoever." (Mahatma Gandhi)

The most pathetic person in the world is someone who has sight, but has no vision. (Helen Keller)

A necessary step on the spiritual journey is for the human person to learn to resist the driving force of the culture in which we live and to become aware of the fact that a person's life can be substantially different than how they might experience it at this moment. A major component of this step is to recognize that the individual person has a choice, the choice to come to an awareness, a deliberate and focused awareness where all your attention is heightened on the everyday events and experiences of your life, from the most profound to the most supposedly inconsequential.[8]

---

[8] Thomas M. Santa, *Sacred Refuge: Why and How to Make a Retreat,* Ave Maria Press (Notre Dame, IN, 2005), page 28.

As you identify less and less with the "me," you will be more at ease with everybody and with everything. Do you know why? Because you are no longer afraid of being hurt or not liked. You no longer desire to impress anyone. Can you imagine the relief when you don't have to impress anybody anymore? Oh, what a relief. Happiness at last! (Anthony de Mello)

CONCLUDING PRAYER

Amazing grace! How sweet the sound
That saved a wretch like me.
I once was lost, but now am found,
Was blind, but now I see.

'Twas grace that taught my heart to fear,
And grace my fears relieved.
How precious did that grace appear
The hour I first believed.

Through many dangers, toils and snares
I have already come;
'Tis grace hath brought me safe thus far
And grace will lead me home.

The Lord has promised good to me
His word my hope secures;
He will my shield and portion be,
As long as life endures.

Yea, when this flesh and heart shall fail,
and mortal life shall cease,
I shall possess within the veil,
A life of joy and peace.

When we've been there ten thousand years
Bright shining as the sun,
We've no less days to sing God's praise
Than when we've first begun.

(Traditional hymn – John Newton)

Monsoon Rain and Grace

Each year during the months of July, August, and September, the Sonoran desert experiences significant rainfall. These seasonal rains are identified as the "monsoon rains" and they serve as a powerful reminder of the power of nature and the ordinary rhythm of life in the desert. When the sky clouds up, the smell of impending moisture begins to fill the air, and the first gusts of wind arrive. When all is in readiness, resident and visitors understand that we will soon experience a real pounding. The rain will swiftly come, the washes will fill up, the road barriers will be dragged from the side of the pavement and placed in position, and the water will run in torrents.

Although I appreciate and stand in awe of the power of the monsoon storms and the electric light show that is often also part of the demonstration, I appreciate even more the gentle rains that we are alternately blessed with. I love listening to the gentle rain as it falls on the roof of my home. I like to stand at a window and watch the rain fall slowly from the sky. I relish the opportunity to search the sky and see if a rainbow or perhaps even two rainbows have formed over the valley.

When such moments occur, I sometimes apply a spiritual lesson to the experience.

I imagine the parched earth of the desert to be a metaphor for my soul while at the same time I imagine the gentle rain as a metaphor for the grace of God poured out. I try and recall the feeling of the desert before the monsoon rains arrive. I remind myself of how much the desert is in need of moisture as the month of May turns into June and the Feast of St. John the Baptist is celebrated. I picture the desert and the desert landscape all the while straining against the burdensome heat of the day, and slowly becoming parched and seemingly lifeless. It is at this moment, when all seems to be in doubt, that the powerful and the gentle rains finally come. I imagine myself in imitation of the desert landscape, stretching out with all of my strength to grab the life-giving water. I imagine the coolness, the healing, and the life-giving strength that is so essential. And then I remind myself that it all comes to me as unearned and unmerited grace, the gift of God.

Perhaps I imagine the spiritual metaphor because it is easier to relate to the metaphor than it is to the actual experience of being a human person in need of the gift of God. Perhaps it is easier to imagine the desert in need of moisture and then make a wonderful spiritual association than it might be to imagine the reality of the everyday experience of my life. I can see the miracle that takes place in the desert. I can recognize the necessity of the life-giving moisture when it arrives, especially when it has been delayed. I can even piously admit that the rain is God's gift of life; however, to go beyond the metaphor and acknowledge the lesson that it teaches is more difficult.

So very often it seems to me I live as a person who believes that I am in need of nothing and no one. I treasure a certain amount of independence. I rely on the many gifts and talents that I have been blessed with. I can sometimes go for long periods of time without any direct reference or acknowledgement of God, even though I am performing many spiritual exercises. And then, suddenly, without warning, I am brought crashing back to the truth that I seem to have so easily ignored.

The straining desert and the monsoon rains are not just a metaphor but also rather something more. The reality of what the desert can teach me if I am willing to listen and to pay attention is all around me. I am the parched desert teetering on the edge of lifelessness. I am in need of the life-giving moisture that can only come as unmerited blessing from God. I need to learn once again with each drop of precious moisture to acknowledge the truth and to become grateful for the gift.

We long for something that is not and shut our eyes to the thing that is. When the Lord Jesus awakens us to reality by new birth and brings us in contact with himself, He does not give us new fathers and mothers and new friends, He gives us new sight. ...It is by coming into contact with the real that we find the ideal. (Oswald Chambers)

"Are you tired? Worn out? Burned out on religion? Come to me. Get away with me and you'll recover your life. I'll show you how to take a real rest. Walk with me and work with me — watch how I do it. Learn the unforced rhythms of grace. I won't lay anything heavy or ill-fitting on you. Keep company with me and you'll learn to live freely and lightly." (Matthew 11:28-30, *The Message* version)

"Jesus does not demand great actions from us but simply surrender and gratitude." (St. Thérèse of the Child Jesus)

In becoming grace, you start from a place of emptiness. When you empty of expectations, you open to the wonders that happen in moments and nanoseconds of revelation. With God's grace active in you, nothing can go wrong. Every thought, word, and action, when joined with grace, will be formless and serve goodness. (Shoni Labowitz, *Miraculous Living*)

CONCLUDING PRAYER

I am, O my God,

but a tiny seed which Thou hast sown

in the soil of Thy love,

and caused to spring forth by the hand of Thy bounty.

This seed craveth, therefore,

in its inmost being,

for the waters of Thy mercy

and the living fountain of Thy grace.

Send down upon it,

from the heaven of Thy loving-kindness,

that which will enable it to flourish beneath Thy shadow

and within the borders of Thy court.

Thou art He Who watereth the hearts of all

that have recognized Thee from Thy plenteous stream

and the fountain of Thy living waters.

Praised be to God,

the Lord of the worlds.

(Baha'i prayers - bahá'u'lláh)

After The Rain

One of my favorite moments in our Sonoran desert occurs after it rains, either the powerful monsoon rains of the summer or one of the infrequent and gentle rains that we experience in the winter. I love going out into the desert and smelling the freshness that seems to fill and permeate my senses. The scent is unlike any other scent that I have ever breathed in. Perhaps it has something of a healing quality to it, or at least I know that I always feel better, no matter what I may have been preoccupied with.

I also enjoy the sound of the desert immediately after the rains come. The desert seems to come alive with the sounds of the birds singing and the busyness of the other creatures. Perhaps it is my imagination, but I even think the rabbits have more of a bounce in their hop, so pleased they seem to be with the gift of moisture. On the blessed occasion when I might glimpse a bobcat or one of our mountain lions, it too seems to be all the more glorious — perhaps as a result of a luxurious bath provided by the rain that washed away the accumulated dirt. Although most of the desert creatures seem to be celebrating, I must admit that the coyotes seem not to be affected by the rain. Coyotes always seem to be busy with something and seemingly unfazed by whatever is happening around them. Perhaps they too are grateful, but they just have a difficult time expressing themselves.

The smells and the desert creatures play an important role in my experience of the desert after a rain, but again it is the mighty saguaro that seems always to capture and focus my attention. The saguaro stands and waits. To the untrained and impatient eye, nothing seems to be happening, but don't let the illusion of no movement fool you and catch you off guard. The many roots of the saguaro that stretch out hundreds, perhaps even a thousand feet, are hard at work. These small roots are frantically occupied, gathering in every droplet of moisture within their reach, to be stored and set aside for the long months where no moisture is possible. The saguaro knows. The saguaro is experienced. The saguaro understands the rhythm of the seasons, the cycle of scarcity and the burst of abundance, which is the way of the Sonoran desert. The saguaro is undoubtedly majestic, but most of all the saguaro seems to be wise.

The spiritual lessons that can be learned from the experience provided by the rain are perhaps obvious, but nevertheless important.

The first lesson is to learn the importance of taking the necessary time to notice the gifts of God that surround us. It is important to breathe in the abundance of God's blessing, to let the breath of God fill us with life. It is important to train our senses so that we can recognize the unbelievable manifestation of the creative power of God that surrounds us, taking nothing for granted. Perhaps we might determine that we will choose a stance in life that is opposite of the coyote, to become focused rather than seemingly unfazed and unmoved.

The second lesson is to learn the wisdom of the saguaro. Our spiritual life is a life that at times will seem to be overflowing with joy and gladness, while still other times we may experience a certain dryness, a perception that God and the gifts of God are far away from us. It is in the moment of dryness, when we are unable to see clearly the activity of God on our behalf, that we become dependent on the reservoir of grace that has been stored within us. It is at the moment of crisis or challenge that we may most need to dig deep within ourselves and be assured that our God is always with us and will never leave us to our own devices. This is a spiritual wisdom that can be learned and practiced so that the truth of our experience of a loving relationship with God is always within our grasp.

Christian, Jew, Muslim, shaman, Zoroastrian, stone, ground, mountain, river, each has a secret way of being with the mystery, unique and not to be judged. (Rumi)

There are only two ways to live your life.
One is as though nothing is a miracle.
The other is as if everything is. (Albert Einstein)

Remain attentive to God, stay utterly dependent on God — this is the lesson of the desert; but it will not transport us away from the desert. (David Rensberger)

Words That Encourage Light and The Spirit of The Lord:
Believing, Calmness, Charity, Cheerful, Contrite, Contrition, Faith, Forgiving, Generous, Gentleness, Giving, Happy, Humility, Joy, Kindness, Long-suffering, Loving, Meekness, Nurturing, Oneness, Openness, Optimistic, Patience, Peaceful, Positive, Prayer, Sacrifice, Selfless, Sharing, Thankful, Trusting, Worship (Author Unknown)

CONCLUDING PRAYER

We bless you Father
for the thirst
you put in us,
for the boldness
you inspire,
for the fire
alight in us
that is you in us,
you the just.

Never mind
that our thirst
is mostly unquenched
(pity the satisfied).
Never mind
our bold plots
are mostly unclinched,
wanted not realized.
Who better than you
knows that success
comes not from us?
You ask us to do
our utmost only,
but willingly.
(Helder Camara)

THE ODE TO JOY

A few years ago a popular movie called Immortal Beloved (1994), a biographical portrayal of Ludwig van Beethoven with the actor Gary Oldman in the title role, made the rounds of the movie theaters. Of the many powerful moments in the story of this great musician, one moment has etched a permanent place in my memory.

According to the story, Beethoven, not yet a teenager, sneaks out of his house one evening when everyone is asleep. He runs down a long deserted road to a small pond, strips off his bedclothes, and dives in. Once in the water he flips over on his back and floats in the pond, surrounded by the brilliance of the stars in the sky, which seem almost to emerge from the water. As we are treated with this picture of the merger of heaven and earth all the while his famous *Ode to Joy* from the Ninth Symphony, the fourth movement, provides the background music and interprets the experience for us. As we share in this intimate moment, we are introduced to the sheer joy and wonder of a creature, surrounded by the handiwork of the Creator. It is almost impossible not to imagine in this moment both Creator and creature who seemingly delight together in the power of the experience.

During the brilliantly clear months of January and February, the scene can be easily duplicated, perhaps not in its entirety, by anyone who is willing to get up a little early from their sleep and emerge into the cool morning. There is something beautiful, I would suggest something sacred, about the Sonoran desert sky this time of year. The stars seem to be at their most brilliant. There is a certain clarity in their placement, an invitation to prayer and meditation that seems to be generated by their light. Perhaps it is the crispness of the morning air that promotes the feeling, but whatever it may be, it can be a powerful experience.

It can become even more powerful if you permit the *Ode to Joy* to work its magic within you. Modern technology enables the experience, and because of the headphone or the small earpiece, the music can be enjoyed without disturbing anyone else and their sleep. If you do not have an MP3 player or some other playback device, the experience can nevertheless be powerful if you simply imagine the music, and let it fill your senses and delight your imagination. If you enjoy the sound of your own voice it is very easy to begin to sing the words, "Jesu joy of man's desiring...."

Some of the most powerful experiences of spirituality emerge, as has been often noted by the spiritual masters, in the experience of silence that we bring to our prayer. However, that being acknowledged as truth, there are other spiritual moments that can also occur when we use some of the other gifts with which God has blessed us.

Beautiful music is one such spiritual gift. Music has the power to lift us up, to transform us. Music can almost effortlessly bring us to the experience of an emotion or feeling that puts us in touch with the sacred presence of God. The music that is created by the great musicians such as Ludwig van Beethoven is certainly one resource, but there is also the music that has been created by lesser-known composers. At the same time it would also be important to recall the concerto that is regularly performed by the creatures of the desert, with the coyote often singing the lead role. The experience of music, however it is enjoyed, can be profound, often leading us to a sacred encounter with our own immortal and beloved.

The presence of God is all around us, calling out to us, probing us, inviting us to pay attention and to enter into relationship. When we learn to recognize the signs of God's presence and respond to God's invitation, the moment becomes for us our own ode to joy. However the connection is made, whatever sense we might use, the experience becomes for each of us a resource that we can return to again and again.

STILLPOINT

God writes the gospel not in the Bible alone,
but on trees and flowers and clouds and stars. (Martin Luther)

All that is in the heavens and the earth glorify God;
And He is the Mighty, the wise.
He is the Sovereignty of the heavens and the earth;
He is able to do all things.
He is the First and the Last,
And the Outward and the Inward;
He is the knower of all things.
(Qur'an LVII:1-3)

Though still in bed, my thoughts go out to you, my Immortal
Beloved, now and then joyfully, then sadly, waiting to learn
whether or not fate will hear us — I can live only wholly with
you or not at all — Yes, I am resolved to wander so long away
from you until I can fly to your arms and say that I am really

at home with you, and can send my soul enwrapped in you into the land of spirits — Yes, unhappily it must be so — You will be the more contained since you know my fidelity to you. No one else can ever possess my heart — never — never — Oh God, why must one be parted from one whom one so loves?
(Ludwig van Beethoven, the *Immortal Beloved* letters)

CONCLUDING PRAYER
The heavens declare the glory of God,
The vault of heaven proclaims his handiwork.
Day discourses of it to day
Night to night hands on the knowledge.

No utterance at all, no speech,
Not a sound to be heard,
But from the entire earth the design stands out,
This message reaches the whole world. (Psalm 19:1-4)